INHERITANCE
the Living Christ is our Living Hope

A STUDY THROUGH 1 PETER

by Marjie Schaefer

www.FlourishThroughTheWord.com

ISBN: 978-1-7328977-1-7
© 2021 by Marjie Schaefer. All rights reserved. No part of this document may be reproduced or transmitted in any form by any means, electronic, mechanical, photocopying, recording, or otherwise, without prior written permission of Marjie Schaefer.

Dedication

This study is dedicated to our loving, merciful, holy, and unchanging God.

This study was written after the world experienced so many changes due to the pandemic. One thing I was reminded of is how all of life may change right in front of my eyes, but the Lord does not change. I am so very thankful for Him and His Word.

In a day and age of so much information and dis-information, we can rest in the truth of God's Word.

I Peter is a book heavy-laden with truth from the one who challenged Jesus. One day, Jesus told His disciples everything that would happen to Him, and Peter immediately said, "No, Lord, this shall not happen." Jesus then looked at Peter and said, "Get behind me satan! You are an offense to Me, for you are not mindful of the things of God, but of the things of men" (Matthew 16:23).

If Jesus said that to one of His very disciples who walked with Him daily for three years, heard every sermon He gave, and witnessed His miracles, how much more can we learn from this statement.

I need to be mindful of the things of God. Spending time in His Word equips me to do that.

The following quote from Martyn Lloyd-Jones has continued to challenge me:

"The more I try to live this Christian life, and the more I read the New Testament, the more convinced I am that the trouble with most of us is that we have never truly realized what it is to be a Christian. If only we understood what the Christian really is and the position in which (s)he is placed, if only we realized the privilege and the possibilities of that position, and above everything, the glorious destiny of everyone who is truly a Christian, then our entire outlook would be completely changed…there are only two groups of people in the world today—those who are of the world and those who belong to Christ….in light of this, it is vital that we should ask ourselves the question: am I of the world or am I not?"

May God pour out His blessing on your study of 1 Peter.

Before you begin...

1 Peter is chock-full of these topics:

- Faith, hope, and love
- Grace
- Trials
- Holiness
- The importance of the Word for daily life
- Loving each other
- Marriage
- Submission
- Employee-employer relationships
- The church

... to name a few!

No matter your status in life, this book has something for you in it! We will spend one week on each chapter, but we are barely dipping our toe into the waters of 1 Peter. This study is designed to be a weekly study on each of the densely-packed chapters, lasting for five weeks in the large group, and five weeks for your personal study to be shared at your discussion groups.

Each day you are given the opportunity to write out the three things you are grateful for. Please take the time to do this. Also included in each week is a Bible study method (see SOAP explanation in the study books) meant to give you the opportunity to dive into a passage on your own and draw out the truth that you can share with others. At the end of each week's study is a solo summary—an opportunity for you to write down your number one take-away from each chapter.

One of the characteristic hallmarks of our studies is the inclusion of traditional hymns, providing you with an opportunity for personal worship.

"But may the God of all grace, who called us to His eternal glory by Jesus Christ, after you have suffered a while, perfect, establish, strengthen, and settle you" (1 Peter 5:10).

To God be the glory,

Marjie

Theme Song for our study in 1 Peter

Living Hope
by Phil Wickham

How great the chasm that lay between us
How high the mountain I could not climb
In desperation, I turned to heaven
And spoke your name into the night
Then through the darkness
Your loving kindness
Tore through the shadows of my soul
The work is finished, the end is written
Jesus Christ, my living hope
Who could imagine so great a mercy?
What heart could fathom such boundless grace?
The God of ages stepped down from glory
To wear my sin and bear my shame
The cross has spoken, I am forgiven
The King of Kings calls me His own
Beautiful Savior, I'm Yours forever
Jesus Christ, my living hope
Hallelujah, praise the One who set me free
Hallelujah, death has lost its grip on me
You have broken every chain
There's salvation in Your name
Jesus Christ, my living hope
Then came the morning that sealed the promise
Your buried body began to breathe
Out of the silence, the roaring lion
Declared the grave has no claim on me
Jesus, Yours is the victory, whoa!
Hallelujah, praise the One who set me free
Hallelujah, death has lost its grip on me
You have broken every chain
There's salvation in Your name
Jesus Christ, my living hope
Jesus Christ, my living hope
Oh God, You are my living hope

(Data from: Musixmatch online)

Week One

Living in Hope
Walking in Holiness

Holy, Holy, Holy

Holy, holy, holy, Lord God Almighty!
Early in the morning our song shall rise to Thee
Holy, holy, holy, merciful and mighty
God in three Persons, blessed Trinity!

Holy, holy, holy, all the saints adore Thee
Casting down their golden crowns around the glassy sea
Cherubim and seraphim falling down before Thee
Which wert, and art, and evermore shalt be

Holy, holy, holy, though the darkness hide Thee
Though the eye of sinful man Thy glory may not see
Only Thou art holy, there is none beside Thee
Perfect in power, in love, and purity!

Holy, holy, holy, Lord God Almighty!
All thy works shall praise Thy name in earth and sky and sea
Holy, holy, holy, merciful and mighty
God in three Persons, blessed Trinity!

Songwriters: Traditional
Data from: Musixmatch

Week One : DAY ONE

Read: 1 Peter 1: 1-25

Prayer: *Dear Lord, speak to me specifically and definitely through Your Word. Guide me through this study and seal these lessons upon my heart. In Jesus' name, amen.*

1. You will find that the first chapter of 1 Peter is 'truth per square inch'! He has much to say to us and there is much for us to process, pray through, and apply. To get a working perspective on this chapter, read through chapter one of 1 Peter three times. As you do, circle or underline these words: hope, faith, and love.

2. From your exercise above, write out one verse from each word that impacted you and share why.

3. From verses 1-2, answer these questions:

    - Who wrote this letter?

    - Write down additional information you know about him.

    - Who was he writing to?

    - Where were they scattered?

    - Do you know why they were scattered?

    - Write out verse two and note all of the prepositional phrases (recall your grammar class).

    - Explain the meaning of elect, foreknowledge, and sanctification.

Your Daily Gratitude List:

Each day you are given the opportunity to write three things you are grateful for. Your challenge is to include one thing you've learned from your time in the Scripture today.

Heaven Anticipated:

What a mercy that Jesus is ever with us, by day, by night, in sickness, in health, in time and through eternity! "I will never leave thee nor forsake thee." But we live in a changing world. The creature changes, we change, but, "I the Lord change not." Ever the same loving, faithful friend is Jesus. Bless the Lord for this, O my soul! I live in Him, and I desire to live for Him and with Him, even here, as far as I can, in the body. But oh, the joy of knowing and feeling, that ere long I shall be with and like Him forever! How great the bliss, even in anticipation of beholding Him face to face! Heaven is a prepared place for a prepared people. Oh the lovingkindness, the tender mercy of Him who lived and died and rose again for us, and whose glory will not be perfect until He has brought His one family around Him, the last elect vessel of mercy led home! This will be the consummation of all things to Him. Then will He rejoice over His Bride with joy unspeakable. I leave it all to Him to unveil as seems good in His sight. ~Heaven Opened, pages 1-2

Week One : DAY TWO

Read 1 Peter 1:3-12 and answer the questions.

Prayer: *Lord, help me to understand my inheritance and the living hope that Jesus makes available to me each day.*

1. Each week, we will be doing a Bible study method that equips and enables you to dig into the scriptures and expand your own understanding.

    Today we launch our S-O-A-P devotions:
    S-write out the verse/passage of scripture that speaks to your heart.
    O-observation: what stood out to you about this passage? Were there any commands or instructions? What is the author saying?
    A-application: How can you apply this passage to your life today? How can you live in light of this truth?
    P-pray: respond to this passage in prayer. Ask God to help you apply this scripture to your life and spend time listening to what He is telling you.

    Do SOAP devotions on 1 Peter 1: 3-5 and be prepared to share your findings with your group.

2. The word "kept" (verse 5), is *phroureo* in Greek (Strong's #5432), which is a military term picturing a sentry standing guard as protection against the enemy. The tense of this verb reveals that we are constantly being guarded by God, giving us assurance that we will one day arrive safely in heaven. Knowing this about that one word, how does this impact your daily life in Christ? How will this change the way you are praying? How can you apply this to something that is causing anxiety in you?

11

3. In verses 6-7, what do you learn about trials? List out all the scriptural lessons here:

4. Faith means surrendering all to God and obeying His word no matter the circumstances we may find ourselves in. From 1 Peter 1:8, write out the three directives we glean from this verse.

5. What do we receive as the outcome of our faith as stated in verse 9?

6. Read verses 10-12 and answer the following:

    • What did the prophets do?

    • Who was it intended for?

    • What did the Spirit reveal to the prophets?

Your Daily Gratitude List:
Each day you are given the opportunity to write three things you are grateful for. Your challenge is to include one thing you've learned from your time in the Scripture today.

Week One : DAY THREE

Read 1 Peter 1: 13-21

Prayer: *Lord, teach me from Your Word what it means to walk in hope and to walk in holiness. Help me to understand how to practically live it out each day.*

1. In verse 13, the word "therefore" reminds us how the assuredness of our salvation (in verses 10-12) is the basis for our holy living. God's Word is very practical. In verses 13-14, practical commands are given to us as we live for Him with the help of the Holy Spirit. Write out what these five practicalities are; the first one is done for you:

    - Prepare my mind for action.

    -

    -

    -

    -

2. We are washed in the blood of Jesus Christ, and this is what makes us holy. Write out verses 15 and 16 here and share the fresh insight you glean from them.

3. Explain in your own words, what it means to walk and to live in practical holiness that reflects our saving relationship with Jesus Christ.

4. The first step towards walking in holiness is to ask, 'What does the Bible say?' 1 Peter 1:16 tells us clearly, "because it is written, 'Be holy, for I am holy.' What do we learn from 1 Peter 1:17-19? Write out truth of these verses here:

5. Read 1 Peter 1: 18-21. From these verses, what can you glean is the highest motive for holy living?

6. When you meditate on the sacrifice of Jesus for you, how does this shape your desire to obey Him and to live for His glory?

Your Daily Gratitude List:
Each day you are given the opportunity to write three things you are grateful for. Your challenge is to include one thing you've learned from your time in the Scripture today.

Week One : DAY FOUR

A STUDY IN HOLINESS

Prayer: *Lord, I desire to be holy as You have commanded and set forth in Your Word. I know that You would never ask me to do something where You have not made a way for me to do it. I want to surrender to You, to learn from You, to gaze upon Your beauty and holiness so that I can be a consistent light for Jesus, one that reflects Your love to every person I meet.*

Holy: pure; set apart; belonging to God. God is holy. He is perfect and without sin. Jesus is holy. He is without sin and dedicated to doing what God wants. Because Jesus died to take the punishment for sin and then rose again, people who believe in Him have the power to be holy too. God helps us to become more and more pure and loving, like Jesus.

1. The Holy Spirit sets us apart for the purpose of obedience and holy living. Look up the following scriptures and answer the questions:

    - 1 Peter 1:2: What is to be our response to what Jesus has done for us?

    - 1 Peter 1:14-16: What are we to understand so that we are empowered to live holy lives?

    - 1 Peter 1:17-19: How do we live in holiness?

2. Look up the following verses and write out what you learn about the Lord and holiness:

    - Isaiah 6:3

    - Romans 14:17

    - 1 Corinthians 2:13

    - Ephesians 1:4

    - Ephesians 1:13

    - 1 John 1:5-10

3. What is the Lord revealing to you as to what holy living looks like in your life?

Your Daily Gratitude List:
Each day you are given the opportunity to write three things you are grateful for. Your challenge is to include one thing you've learned from your time in the Scripture today.

Week One : DAY FIVE

Read 1 Peter 1: 22-25

Prayer: *Lord, thank You for my salvation through the work of Jesus Christ. As I end this week of study, help me to learn more from Your incorruptible Word and to love those You have placed in my path.*

1. What does the Lord call us to do in verse 22?

2. How can we practically and authentically obey that command?

3. Verse 23 is an incredible verse in that it sets forth the significance of God's Word in our lives. To gain greater clarity, look up 1 Thessalonians 2:13 and James 1:18 and write out each one along with 1 Peter 1:23. Summarize what the Bible reveals about the Word and our lives.

4. We are told in verse 23 that the 'Word of God lives and abides forever', since that is the absolute truth, tell how you make God's Word a daily priority in your life?

5. God's Word has the power to bring spiritual life to all who open it. Read verses 1 Peter 1:24-25 and summarize the truth gleaned from these verses.

Your Daily Gratitude List:
Each day you are given the opportunity to write three things you are grateful for. Your challenge is to include one thing you've learned from your time in the Scripture today.

Solo Summary:
Write out your number one take-away from this chapter of study.

"Lord and God, You are worthy to receive glory and honor and power, for You created all things. You created me and adopted me as Your child through Jesus Christ, in accordance with Your pleasure and will. I pray that I may be active in sharing my faith, so I will have a full understanding of every good thing I have in Christ.

Father, I ask You to give me a complete understanding of what You want to do in my life, and I ask You to make me wise with spiritual wisdom. Then the way I live will always honor and please You, and I will continually do good, kind things for others. All the while, I will learn to know You better and better.

I roll my works upon You, Lord, and You make my thoughts agreeable to Your will, so my plans are established and succeed. You direct my steps and make them sure. I understand and firmly grasp what the will of the Lord is for I am not vague, thoughtless, or foolish. I stand firm and mature in spiritual growth, convinced and fully assured in everything You will.

Thank You, Father, for the Holy Spirit who abides permanently in me and who guides me into all the truth."

~Prayers that Avail Much, page 65

Week Two

Daily Walking In the Word

Ancient words

Holy words long preserved
For our walk in this world
They resound with God's own heart
Oh, let the Ancient words impart
Words of Life, words of Hope
Give us strength, help us cope
In this world, where e'er we roam
Ancient words will guide us Home
Ancient words ever true
Changing me, and changing you
We have come with open hearts
Oh, let the ancient words impart
Holy words of our Faith
Handed down to this age
Came to us through sacrifice
Oh, heed the faithful words of Christ
Holy words long preserved
For our walk in this world
They resound with God's own heart
Oh, let the ancient words impart
Ancient words ever true
Changing me, and changing you
We have come with open hearts
Oh, let the ancient words impart
Ancient words ever true
Changing me, and changing you
We have come with open hearts
Oh, let the ancient words impart

~Freeman and Wood;
Capital Christian Music Group; LyricFind

Week Two : DAY ONE

Read 1 Peter 2:1-8

Prayer: *Lord, thank You for Your Word which gives me daily nourishment as I seek to walk with You. Speak to me now as I study and teach me new things out of Your living and active Word.*

1. Why do you read the Bible?

2. Genuine love for brothers and sisters in Christ, as well as an ongoing desire for the Word of God not only go together, but they also result in spiritual growth. Read 1 Peter 1:25 along with 1 Peter 2:1-3 and share how relationships and a thirst for God's Word cause growth.

3. What is a practical thing you can do if you find you do not have a consistent hunger or desire for the Word of God?

4. Peter warns of our need to lay aside certain wrong attitudes of the heart that can hinder our spiritual growth. List those out of 1 Peter 2:1 and define what each one means.

5. Peter gave a full description of Jesus Christ, our chief cornerstone of the church, in 1 Peter 2:4. What are the three ways Peter described Jesus in this verse?

6. Visit Isaiah 28:16 and Psalm 118:22 and share a further description of Jesus from these verses.

7. In His first mention of the church, Jesus compared it to a building: "I will build my church" (Matthew 16:18). Believers are living stones in His building. Read and record the lessons you glean from Ephesians 2:19-22 and compare it to 1 Peter 2:4-6.

8. Jesus was not the kind of Messiah the Jewish people were expecting, so they stumbled over Him. In 1 Peter 2:7-8, tell the reasons why the people stumbled over Jesus, and be specific.

Your Daily Gratitude List:
Each day you are given the opportunity to write three things you are grateful for. Your challenge is to include one thing you've learned from your time in the Scripture today.

Week Two : DAY TWO

Read 1 Peter 2:9-12

Prayer: *Lord, I'm so thankful that You chose me!! What a gift and a privilege to be a part of Your church–the habitation of God through the Holy Spirit. Thank You for giving me life in You.*

1. The description of the church in these verses in 1 Peter 2, parallels God's description of Israel in Exodus 19:5-6 and Deuteronomy 7:6. Write out these verses and show the parallel. How is the church today shining a light for the Lord in our world?

2. In 1 Peter 2:9, privileges are listed for the people of God. Write each one out here:

3. A chosen generation speaks to the grace of God. Look up Deuteronomy 7:7-8 and John 15:16 to write out the scriptural truth of being chosen.

4. We have been set apart to belong exclusively to God. Look up Philippians 3:20 and Leviticus 10:10 and write out the scriptural truth of being a holy nation.

5. We are the people of God. Write out the truth of Ephesians 2:1-3 and 11-19 and tell how we once were before the Lord redeemed us.

6. Based on this truth and goodness found in verse 9, how are we to respond?

7. 1 Peter 2:11-12 gives us additional specifics for living a holy life in a world that does not know Jesus. Write those out here and pray over them, asking God to point out anything in you that is not reflective of Him.

8. As you wrap up today's study, take some time to truly worship the Lord—praising Him for choosing you, for His deliverance through the blood of the Lamb, and for His equipping of you through the power of the Holy Spirit and His Word. Write out your prayer of praise to God or play your favorite worship song; sing the hymns provided for you in the study book. The Lord is worthy of our praise!

(THIS TIME OF WORSHIP IS IN PLACE OF YOUR DAILY GRATITUDE TODAY.)

Week Two : DAY THREE

Read 1 Peter 2: 13-17

Prayer: *Lord, help me to remember that I am a representative of Jesus Christ everywhere I go. Help me to live out each day the truth of Your Word. Write it upon my heart and cause me to remember Your truths as I live and breathe.*

1. Write out 1 Peter 2:13. Look up Matthew 22:16-21 and share how Jesus approached the government of man.

2. Is it possible to submit to government or institutions and still disobey the laws? Why or why not? Use Scripture to support your answer.

3. Read Daniel 1 and explain how Daniel and his friends refused to obey the king's dietary rules yet still honored the king.

4. Peter faced a challenge after Pentecost when he was told to stop preaching by the Jewish council. (Read all about it in Acts 4-5.) Tell exactly what happened from Acts 4:18-21 and 5:29.

5. How do these two biblical stories highlight the truth of 1 Peter 2:13-17?

6. In 1 Peter 2:15 and 16, what are the two important phrases that you see in the text?

Your Daily Gratitude List:
Each day you are given the opportunity to write three things you are grateful for. Your challenge is to include one thing you've learned from your time in the Scripture today.

Week Two : DAY FOUR

Read 1 Peter 2: 18-21

Prayer: *Lord, help me to understand Your Word and how it relates to me today. Help me to remember that it has all been preserved for me as I live in this century. Your Word is living and active and meant to speak to me today.*

1. There are no Christian slaves today, at least not in the New Testament sense. Peter gave application for employees. We are to be submissive to those who are over us, whether they are kind or unkind. Each worker is to honor God by his work ethic and his attitude on the job.

    Use the SOAP devotions for verses 18-21 in this passage. Be prepared to share your insights with your group.

    > **S**-write out the passage of scripture.
    > **O**-observation: what stood out to you about these verses? Were there any commands or instructions? What is the author saying?
    > **A**-application: How can you apply this passage to your life today? How can you live in light of this truth?
    > **P**-pray: respond to this passage in prayer. Ask God to help you apply this scripture to your life and spend time listening to what He is telling you.

2. 1 Peter 2:21 tells us that Jesus left us an example for us to follow. "Example", the Greek word, *hupogrammos*, Strong's #5261: From *hupo* when means under, and *grapho*, which means to write, an underwriting. The word referred to tracing letters or copying the writing of a teacher. It came to denote an example to follow. At this point in your study, write out how you've learned more from the example of Jesus and how this is impacting your daily walk with Him.

Your Daily Gratitude List:
Each day you are given the opportunity to write three things you are grateful for. Your challenge is to include one thing you've learned from your time in the Scripture today.

Week Two : DAY FIVE

Read 1 Peter 2:22-25

Prayer: *Lord, I thank You for the lessons of 1 Peter so far. You are showing me through Your Word that Jesus left me an example I can follow, and how my circumstances are not meant to affect my daily walk with Him. Life may be hard at times, but Jesus is my example. Continue to teach me through Your Word today.*

1. Re-read 1 Peter 2:21 as a reminder of the context Peter is giving to each of us. All that Jesus did on earth, as recorded in the Gospels, is a perfect example for us to follow. He is especially an example for us in the way He responded to suffering. List out what you learn from Jesus in verses 22-23.

2. Jesus proved that we could be in the will of God, be greatly loved by God, and still suffer unjustly. Our Lord's humility and submission were not an evidence of weakness but of power. Read and write out your insights from John 18:33-38.

3. Christ is our Redeemer. In I Peter 2:24-25, write out the Gospel message from these verses in such a way that you could easily share it with someone who is searching for truth.

4. Peter shares with us the Christian conversion experience from verses 24-25. Look up Isaiah 53:5 and show why Peter included this verse in his explanation.

Your Daily Gratitude List:

Solo Summary:
Write out your number one take-away from this chapter of study.

To walk in the Word

Father, in the Name of Jesus, I commit myself to walk in the Word. Your Word living in me produces Your life in this world. I recognize that Your Word is integrity itself—steadfast, sure, eternal—and I trust my life to its provisions.

You have sent Your Word forth into my heart. I let it dwell in me richly in all wisdom. I meditate in it day and night so that I may diligently act on it. The incorruptible seed, the Living Word, the Word of Truth is abiding in my spirit. That seed is growing mightily in me now, producing Your nature, Your life. It is my counsel, my shield, my powerful weapon in battle. The Word is a lamp to my feet and a light to my path. It makes my way plain before me. I do not stumble, for my steps are ordered in the Word.

The Holy Spirit leads and guides me into all the truth. He gives me understanding, discernment, and comprehension so that I am preserved from the snares of the evil one.

I delight myself in You and Your Word. Because of that, You put Your desires within my heart. I commit my way unto You, and You bring it to pass. I am confident that You are at work in me now both to will and to do all Your good pleasure.

I exalt Your Word, hold it in high esteem and give it first place. I make my schedule around Your Word. I make the Word the final authority to settle all questions that conform me. I choose to agree with the Word of God, and I choose to disagree with any thoughts, conditions, or circumstances contrary to Your Word. I boldly and confidently say that my heart is fixed and established on the solid foundation—the living Word of God! Amen. (From Prayers that Avail Much, pages. 67-68)

Week Three

I Surrender All

I surrender all

All to Jesus, I surrender
All to Thee I freely give
I will ever love and trust You
In Your presence daily live
I surrender all, I surrender all
All to Thee, my blessed Savior
I surrender all

All to Jesus, I surrender
Lord, I give myself to Thee
Fill me with Your love and power
Let Your blessing fall on me
I surrender all, I surrender all
All to Thee, my blessed Savior
I surrender all

All to Jesus I surrender
Now I feel the sacred flame
O the joy of full salvation
Glory, glory, to Your name

I surrender all, I surrender all
All to Thee, my blessed Savior
I surrender all (I surrender all)
I surrender all, I surrender all
All to Thee, my blessed Savior
I surrender all

(From Musicmatch online)

Week Three : DAY ONE

Read all of 1 Peter 3 today
Focus verses: 1 Peter 3: 1-7

Prayer: *Lord, thank You for the lessons You have provided for me from Peter, the disciple who was with Jesus and saw His miracles and heard His messages. Help me to learn from Your Word today as I study these verses.*

1. No matter your marital status, you can learn from the Word the essentials for a godly marriage relationship. The opening phrase or wording of verse one is meant to refer us back to Peter's discussion on Jesus' example in 1 Peter 2:21-25. Before we jump in to his 'word to the wives', go back and read these verses in 1 Peter 2, and write out the lessons you glean from them.

2. The "S" word has become somewhat of a difficult one for our modern society. How many times does Peter remind Christian wives to be submissive to their own husbands in this passage?

3. The word submission has to do with order and authority, not evaluation of value. In other words, we learn how God has a place for everything and has ordained various levels of authority. Submission does not mean that the wife is inferior to the husband. There is nothing degrading about submitting to or accepting God's order. Read again, 1 Peter 2:13-14, along with Ephesians 5:21. Use these along with our passage for today, and give three reasons why a Christian wife is called to biblically submit to her husband, even if the husband is not saved.

4. What did Peter make clear in 1 Peter 3:7?

5. Explain how Genesis 1:28 and Galatians 3:28 confirm Peter's conclusion in 1 Peter 3:7.

Your Daily Gratitude List:
If you're married, today's a good day to list some things you're grateful to God for about your husband. If you're not married, express your gratitude to God for the godly examples of marriage that you see around you.

Week Three : DAY TWO

Read 1 Peter 3:1-7 again for today

Prayer: *Lord, help me to learn everything You have for me in this section of scripture. I want my life to consistently characterize Jesus in everything I do.*

1. In 1 Peter 3:3-6, specific instructions are given to wives, but no matter your status in life, there are powerful principles for us to glean from these four verses. These verses reveal to us that a quiet confidence, not from intimidation, but from the fruit of trusting in God, yields godly 'adornment'. Use today's vernacular to describe what a 'gentle and quiet spirit' means or looks like for all women.

2. From this passage, we see the greatest value placed on the inner beauty of the heart, one that reflects a peaceful and humble spirit. Again, we look at the example of Jesus. Use Matthew 21:5 along with this Greek word and translation to express the beauty of a heart that is precious to God: *praus*, Strong's #4235—a humility that is considerate, unassuming, gentle, mild, meek. Jesus showed a greater power than armed might, the power of humble wisdom and love. Meekness is not weakness, but power under control.

3. Peter used the Old Testament example of Sarah to encourage all women today. Read Genesis 18 and write out what you learn from Sarah's life. Although she was imperfect (like all of us), she is who Peter pointed out as another example for us.

4. Because the Christian women of his day were experiencing a new situation and new freedoms, Peter devoted more time and space to instructing wives. In verse 7, Peter did list four areas of responsibility to husbands. List them here:

5. A personal note: I am not a huge fan of reading marriage books. My personal conviction is that married Christian couples have an obligation to keep Jesus at the center of their personal lives, and thus, at the center of their marriage. The best marriage book is the Bible! That being said, here are two helpful and Biblically-sound books on marriage that I have read:

   • **Sacred Marriage** (what if God designed marriage to make us holy more than to make us happy?) by Gary Thomas

   • **Love and Respect**, by Dr. Emerson Eggerichs.

   "A magnificent marriage begins not with knowing one another but with knowing God."
   ~Gary and Betsy Ricucci

Your Daily Gratitude List:

Week Three : DAY THREE

Read 1 Peter 3: 8-12

Prayer: *Lord, help me to love all the people You have placed in my life as this is what You have called me to. Enable and equip me to be compassionate and a blessing to everyone I meet.*

1. Love is a theme that shows up over and over again in Peter's letter. List out the evidences of love as seen in verse 8.

2. Jesus showed us the godly response to enemies in 1 Peter 2:23. Peter himself had to learn the hard way how to respond to his enemies—see Luke 22:47-53 for the story. Write the specifics of loving an enemy as stated in 1 Peter 3: 9.

3. 1 Peter 3:10-12 gives us a formula for 'seeing good days'. Write out the four positive approaches to life we can take as believers listed in these verses. How are you doing in each area? Take some time to pray over these today before wrapping up this day of study.

4. Have you had a 'bad day' recently? Peter encouraged us to look for good days in this passage. He was quoting Psalm 34. Finish your study today by reading it out loud as a benediction and a fresh commitment to love life and to look for God's blessings and His nearness to you.

Your Daily Gratitude List:

Week Three : DAY FOUR

Read 1 Peter 3: 13-17

Prayer: *Lord, I'm so grateful that You're teaching me through the writings of Peter that the fear of the Lord conquers every other fear. Help me to continue to 'set apart Christ as Lord' in my heart each moment of each day.*

1. This section of Peter's letter discusses God's grace in suffering. To understand more of the context of what he wrote in this section, read Isaiah 8:13-14 and write down the specific lessons gleaned from these verses.

2. Based on 1 Peter 3:13-15, what are the two responses to suffering that Peter gives?

3. Instead of experiencing fear as we face an enemy, we can experience blessing if Jesus is Lord in our hearts. The word "happy" in verse 14 is the same as "blessed" in Matthew 5:10. Look up that verse, along with 1 Peter 1:8, and tell how each trial or suffering becomes an opportunity to share the reality of Jesus with others.

4. As believers study the Word, we better understand the will of God and our conscience becomes more sensitive to right and wrong. Based on verses 16-17, explain how a good conscience helps a believer in times of trial and opposition.

Inscribed on Martin Luther's monument in Germany are his courageous words spoken before the church council on April 18, 1521:

"Here I stand; I can do no other. God help me. Amen."
His conscience, bound to God's Word, gave him the courage
to defy those who were not honoring God's ways.

Your Daily Gratitude List:

Week Three : DAY FIVE

Read 1 Peter 3: 18-22

Prayer: *Thank You, Lord, that Your Word is life, even when I come across difficult-to-understand passages. Help me to rightly handle the Word of truth as I dig deeper and seek to process and glean what You have for me in today's passage.*

When Peter wrote this section of his letter, he had no idea that it would be classified as one of the most difficult portions of the New Testament! Interpreters have wrestled for years as to what is meant in this passage.

We may not be able to understand everything found in this section, but we do want to get the practical help that Peter gave to encourage Christians in difficult days.

One of the most beneficial things we can do as we study this passage, is to dig in for ourselves and utilize the SOAP devotional form of study for these five verses.

Your study for today is to apply this method on this passage and to glean the practical application for yourself as you unpack it. Be prepared to discuss and share this with your group.

> **S**-write out the passage of scripture.
> **O**-observation: what stood out to you about this passage? Were there any commands or instructions? What is the author saying?
> **A**-application: How can you apply this passage to your life today? How can you live in light of this truth?
> **P**-pray: respond to this passage in prayer. Ask God to help you apply this scripture to your life and spend time listening to what He is telling you.

YOUR DAILY GRATITUDE LIST:
Each day you are given the opportunity to write three things you are grateful for. Your challenge is to include one thing you've learned from your time in the Scripture today.

Solo Summary:
Write out your number one take-away from this chapter of study.

Week Four

Ready, Waiting, Willing And Available

Blessed Assurance

Blessed assurance, Jesus is mine
Oh, what a foretaste of glory divine
Heir of salvation, purchase of God
Born of His spirit and washed in His blood
This is my story, this is my song
Praising my Savior all the day long
This is my story, this is my song
Praising my Savior all the day long
Perfect submission, perfect delight
Visions of rapture now burst on my sight
Angels descending, bring from above
Echoes of mercy and whispers of love
This is my story, this is my song
Praising my Savior all the day long
This is my story, this is my song
Praising my Savior all the day long
Perfect submission, all is at rest
I, in my Savior, am happy and blessed
Watching and waiting, looking above
Filled with His goodness and lost in His love
This is my story, this is my song
Praising my Savior all the day long
This is my story, this is my song
Praising my Savior all the day long

Written by Fanny J. Crosby
Taken from Musicmatch online

Week Four : DAY ONE

Read all of 1 Peter 4 today
Focus verses: 1 Peter 4: 1-6

Prayer: *Thank You Lord for the practical messages in Your Word. Help me to daily cultivate a healthy outlook on my life here on earth and the impact I can have on eternity.*

1. In verses 1 and 2, we are reminded that because Jesus suffered, believers are to be prepared to follow Him in suffering. This has a distilling effect on our mind, will, and emotions, enabling us to live for the will of God.

    - Use 1 Peter 2:21 & 3:18 and explain why Jesus had to suffer.

    - What is our attitude to be towards sin as stated in Romans 6:11?

    - What goal should we strive for based on 1 John 2:28-3:9? Will we ever achieve this goal?

2. In verse 3, Peter is making a point to his listeners that it is helpful to remember who we were before we met Christ. The 'will of the gentiles' means the will of the unsaved world (see 1 Peter 2:12). What can we learn from this verse, and why was it important for Peter to point out this list of behaviors?

3. In verses 4-6, Peter is explaining to us how the unsaved think. They do not understand the radical change that Jesus brings when others trust Christ as Savior. Use 2 Corinthians 4:3-4 and Ephesians 2:1 to help you explain what our attitude should be toward the unsaved.

4. Explain what Peter meant in verse 6 using 1 Peter 1:12; 3:19; Romans 8:9-13, and Galatians 5:25.

Your Daily Gratitude List:

"Live every day as if the Son of Man were at the door, and gear your thinking to the fleeting moment. Just how can it be redeemed? Walk as if the next step would carry you across the threshold of heaven. Pray. That saint who advances on his knees never retreats." ~Jim Elliot

Week Four : DAY TWO

Read 1 Peter 4:7-19

Prayer: *Father, enable me each day to be serious and watchful in my prayers, with a heart towards eternity and the day approaching to be with You. Enable and equip me through Your precious Holy Spirit to love others, show hospitality, and steward the grace of God well. For Your glory, Amen.*

1. The believers in the early church truly expected Jesus to return in their lifetime. I've been here on this earth and a Christian long enough to have witnessed many in that same category! Only the Father knows when He will send His Son back to get us and take us home forever with Him. The important thing is that one day we will all see the Lord and will stand before Him. This attitude of expectancy is meant to create a sense of urgency and zeal for Him as we spend each day on earth. Studying the Bible in a line-upon-line study like this one is one of the most practical and profound things we can do as we wait. Earlier in the study you were asked, 'Why do you read the Bible?' This question will hopefully help you to answer that with more clarity.

    Peter gave 'ten commandments' to his readers in order to help them be ready as they waited. This includes us too! Use the verses listed below from 1 Peter 4 and write out Peter's 'ten commandments':

    - Verse 7

    - Verse 7

    - Verse 8

    - Verse 9

    - Verses 10-11

    - Verse 12

    - Verse 13

    - Verses 15-16

    - Verses 16-18

    - Verse 19

2. Based on your own study and Bible knowledge, choose two and explain what they mean.

Your Daily Gratitude List:

Week Four : DAYS THREE AND FOUR

Read 1 Peter 4: 1-19

Prayer: *Lord, I'm so thankful You preserved Your Word for us so that we have access to Your heart and mind for our daily life while on this earth. Continue to teach me through Your Word today.*

Chapter 4 of 1 Peter begins the way Chapter 3 ends—Peter points to the cross and our blameless, suffering Savior. Peter's letter is an ongoing reminder to us that it is time! It's time to be self-controlled, clear-minded, and standing in the grace of Jesus as we live for His glory! It is time to honor God in all we do, as we live by His grace. Peter does not give us a to-do list, but he is reminding us how we are free to walk and live the reality of all Jesus has done and is doing for us. This is what matters for eternity.

Peter describes four attitudes that a Christian can cultivate for a lifetime. Take a moment to ask God to give you the attitudes that reflect Him before you begin these next two days of study.

1. **A biblical attitude toward sin**—1 Peter 4:1-3:
    A picture is painted in these verses of a soldier who puts on his equipment and gets armed for battle.

    What did sin do to Jesus as seen in verse one?

    Why did Jesus have to suffer? Use 1 Peter 2:21 and 3:18 to help you answer.

    How does enjoying the will of God equip us for life, burdens, and temptations? Use Scripture as you answer.

    Explain how looking back on who we were prior to coming to Christ can be helpful. Romans 6:11 tells us how to think and live. What does 'reckon' mean?

2. **A patient attitude toward the lost**—1 Peter 4:4-6:

    Why is our ongoing engagement with lost people important? Use 1 Peter 3:15 to help you answer.

    Interpret 1 Peter 4:6 in regards to sharing the Gospel with those who do not know Jesus.

    What attitude did Jesus take as seen in 1 Peter 2:23?

    Write out what you learn from Paul's instructions in 2 Timothy 2:24-26. Take a moment to pray for specific people in your life who do not yet know Jesus as Lord and Savior.

3. **An expectant attitude toward Jesus**—1 Peter 4:7
    The opposite of being sober-minded is 'frenzy, madness'. The Greek word *mania* is now part of our vocabulary and psychology. Being sober-minded means we face things realistically and free from delusion. All the more reason to be daily in His Word. The sober-minded Christian will have a purposeful life, not drifting or living without restraint.

    Ten times in his writings, Paul encouraged us to be sober-minded. Look up the following verses and write out more of what you learn about this attitude you can continue to prayerfully cultivate.

    Titus 2:1-6

    Luke 12:31-48

    Romans 13:11

Romans 14:10-23

James 5:8-9

1 Thessalonians 5:6-8

Mark 14:37-40

4. **A fervent attitude toward the believers**—1 Peter 4:8-19
   As we prayerfully cultivate these attitudes, we are to think of others and properly relate to them. Love is truly the badge of a believer in this world.

   The word "fervent" pictures an athlete training to reach her goal and speaks of an eagerness and intensity. Loving others requires prayer, training, and intentionality on our part.

   Write out what Jesus told all of His followers in John 13:34-35.

   Peter quotes Proverbs 10:12 in this section. Write this verse out and explain what it means. Do we get to condone sin based on this verse? Explain why or why not.

   Our hospitality is a reflection of God's heart and hospitality to us. Read Acts 28:7, Philemon 22, 1 Timothy 3:2, and Titus 1:8 and tell why hospitality is a biblical value each of us are called to embrace.

Use Scripture to explain how Christian love results in serving others. How are we to faithfully steward the gifts the Lord has entrusted us with?

Explain what is meant in 1 Peter 4:11. Use other scriptures to help you answer.

Your Daily Gratitude List:
Be sure and list people you are grateful for and ways you have personally experienced their love at work in your life.

"We are all products of our theology. What we believe, or don't believe, about God shows up every day. Sound theology produces sound thinking and living." ~Susan Hunt

Week Four: DAY FIVE

Read 1 Peter 4: 12-19

Prayer: *Lord, thank You for the lessons in Chapter 4 of this book. I ask that You continue to seal them on my heart. Help me to respond to trials and suffering that You allow to touch my life in such a way that glorifies You and releases Your gospel message to the world.*

Did you know that the word Christian is found only three times in the New Testament? I Peter 4:16 is one of those places.

As we come to the end of this chapter, today you will be studying on your own, using the SOAP method again. We've spent several days camping out and unpacking this chapter, but today, you will be looking at what Peter had to say about persecution and suffering. In verse 12, he shows us how we are to expect it. In verses 13-14, he challenges us to rejoice in the midst of it. Peter wraps up this section by encouraging us to examine our lives as we go through the refining process, and he ends by encouraging us to entrust ourselves to our faithful Father. Be ready to share your insights with your group.

> **S**-write out the passage of scripture.
> **O**-observation: what stood out to you about these verses? Were there any commands or instructions? What is the author saying?
> **A**-application: How can you apply this passage to your life today? How can you live in light of this truth?
> **P**-pray: respond to this passage in prayer. Ask God to help you apply this scripture to your life and spend time listening to what He is telling you.

Your Daily Gratitude List:
Each day you are given the opportunity to write three things you are grateful for. Your challenge is to include one thing you've learned from your time in the Scripture today.

Solo Summary:
Write out your number one take-away from this chapter of study.

"The gospel is big enough, good enough and powerful enough to make every moment of every season of life significant and glorious."
~Susan Hunt

Week Five

Submit to God
Resist the devil

You are worthy of it all

All the saints and angels bow before Your throne
All the elders cast their crowns before the Lamb of God and sing

You are worthy of it all,
You are worthy of it all
For from You are all things,
And to You are all things,
You deserve the glory

Day and night, night and day, let incense arise
Day and night, night and day, let incense arise
Day and night, night and day, let incense arise
Day and night, night and day, let incense arise

By David Brymer
AZ Lyrics online

Week Five : DAY ONE

Read all of 1 Peter 5 today
Focus verses: 1 Peter 5: 1-4

Prayer: *Lord, thank You for Peter's final word to us, Your people. Speak to me now as I dive into this final week of study and teach me what You have for me through Your Word.*

Our heavenly Father is the "Lord of heaven and earth" (see Matthew 11:25) and because of that, we have no need to worry. He is faithful and will not fail.

As Peter ended Chapter 4, he wrote: "For the time has come for judgment to begin at the house of God; and if it begins with us first, what will be the end of those who do not obey the gospel of God?" (1Peter 4:17 NKJV).

If judgment is to begin in the house of God, it's important for the Lord's house, or the church, to be in right relationship with God and in order. This is why Peter wrote this special message to the leaders of the church. His desire was to encourage them to do their work faithfully, and to provide spiritual leadership for the 'flock'.

The New Testament church was organized under the leadership of elders and deacons. The words "elder" and "bishop" refer to the same office (Acts 20: 17, 28). The word bishop is often translated to overseer. Please refer to 1 Peter 5:2 and also 1 Peter 2:25 to see it applied to Christ.

Peter was concerned that the leadership in the local churches be at its best. When the trials came, the believers in the churches would look to their elders for encouragement and direction.

Before you decide that this passage doesn't apply to you because you're not an elder or hold a staff position at your church, consider the aspect of shepherding, or caring for the spiritual well-being of those within your circle of influence.

Are you a mother? Then shepherding is a part of your job description.

Are you a grandmother, aunt, sister, cousin, daughter, or friend? As you care for others in the organic relationships of life, shepherding is definitely something all believers are called to do.

While we will be looking at the biblical call to elders and shepherds of the flock, keep in mind your own relationships both at home and in your community. What can you learn?

1. Peter had personal experiences with Jesus, yet he introduced himself as another elder. How does 1 Peter 5:1 remind us of Peter's experiences with Jesus as seen in Matthew 17:1-5, 2 Peter 1:15-18, and John 21:15-17?

2. What is the warning Peter gives in 1 Peter 5:3? How does it align with conversations he had with Jesus in Luke 22:24-30?

3. The image of the flock is often used in the Bible. We were once stray sheep, but the Good Shepherd found us and restored us to the fold. Sheep are clean animals and tend to flock together; they are defenseless and need their shepherd to protect them. What are the four responsibilities Peter lists for the shepherd/elders of their flock as seen in these verses?

4. Based on your answers to number 3 above, write out what each one means for you personally. How can you apply it to your own life?

5. After briefly studying this passage, how will it affect the way you pray for the leadership of your own church? Consider writing a note of encouragement to your pastor or elders. Use this question to also list your gratitude for the spiritual leadership in your life.

Your Daily Gratitude List:

Week Five : DAY TWO

Read 1 Peter 5: 5-11

Prayer: *Lord, thank You for this powerful section of Peter's letter that lists several imperatives for me to obey. Enable me, by Your powerful Holy Spirit, to listen and to obey. Help me to be a humble light for You each day.*

1. Peter gave the church three powerful admonitions to obey if they were to glorify God. List the three out here with the verses and explain what each one means.

2. Peter had already encouraged the church to be submissive. Next to each reference, list the imperative regarding submission and list the current one seen in this section:

    - 1 Peter 2:13-17:

    - 1 Peter 2: 18-25:

    - 1 Peter 3: 1-7:

    - 1 Peter 5:5-7:

3. Peter really knew his Old Testament! Write out the verse he quotes to defend his point in Proverbs 3:34.

4. Tell why God resists the proud and use these verses to answer: Proverbs 6:16-17; Proverbs 8:13; Isaiah 14:12-15; 1 John 2:16.

5. Why is submission an act of faith?

6. What have you learned about biblical submission throughout this study and how can you tie it all in with the wonderful promise of 1 Peter 5:6? How is 'due time' different from your time?

Your Daily Gratitude List:
Each day you are given the opportunity to write three things you are grateful for. Your challenge is to include one thing you've learned from your time in the Scripture today.

"God reveals Himself to us in His Word. Our flourishing happens in proportion to time spent getting to know Him through His Word. An ever-growing knowledge of God produces a more mature, God-centered perspective on our identity and purpose..." ~Susan Hunt

Week Five : DAY THREE

Read 1 Peter 5: 7-14

Prayer: *Lord, help me, by Your grace and power, to give all of my cares- past, present, and future—to You once and for all. Remind me of this powerful scripture and how this is Your desire for me- to walk in freedom and wholeness in Jesus, because He cares for me.*

1. The word "care" in the Greek is *merimna*; Strong's #3308; from *meiro*, 'to divide', and *noos*, 'the mind'. The word denotes distractions, anxieties, burdens and worries. *Merimna* means to be anxious beforehand about daily life. Such worry is unnecessary because the Father's love provides for both our daily needs and our special needs.

   How amazing to see this word in the Greek and to learn that worry actually divides our minds. And Peter made sure, before he ended this portion of his letter, that he reminded God's people to give it all to Him—there's no need for us to be distracted or divided in our minds. If anyone knew from experience that God cares for His own, it was Peter! Look up the following verses and tell how Jesus cared for Peter in each one:

   - Mark 1: 29-31

   - Luke 5: 1-11

   - Matthew 17: 24-27

   - Matthew 14:22-33

   - Luke 22:50-51

   - Acts 12

2. How does God show His love and care for us when we give our cares to Him? Look up each Scripture and tell how:

   - Isaiah 41:10

   - James 1:5

   - Philippians 4:13

   - Psalm 37:5

   - Psalm 55:22

3. Each one of us will experience anxiety and care in our daily lives, it's what we do with it that impacts our relationship with Jesus and our witness to a fallen world. One of the reasons why you have been asked each day to list your gratitude through this study is so that you could see on paper how the Lord is caring for you in real time. End this lesson by writing out your gratitude and thanking Him for His care of you today.

If you happen to be dealing with anxiety at this time, try writing those needs/cares on separate pieces of paper and one-by-one casting them onto the Lord. Then rip up the papers and throw them away! If they start to gnaw on your mind again, remind yourself that you have given them to God once and for all.

Your Daily Gratitude List:

"In all His dealings, whatever they may be, there is nothing but the tenderest love towards you, all designed to draw you nearer and nearer to Himself. Forget not that it is through much tribulation we are to enter the kingdom; but it is all to prepare us for the fuller enjoyment of it when we arrive there. Wait patiently, looking unto Jesus, trusting Him fully for all things, within and without. O, this is sweet living—living upon Christ! He cares for you. You need not trouble yourself about or load yourself with earthly cares. Carry them, as they arise to Him and do not set yourself about to manage matters, when He, who has sent the cares, will manage better for you than you can for yourself. Trust Him, wholly trust Him." ~Heaven Opened

Week Five : DAY FOUR

Read 1 Peter 5: 8-14

Prayer: *Your Word reminds me that I have an enemy who desires to see me destroyed. Thank You that he is defeated and You are my victory. Continue to teach me through Your Word.*

1. What are the imperatives in 1 Peter 5: 8? Write them down.

2. The devil is a dangerous enemy and it is important for us to know his abilities. Look up these verses that inform you of your enemy and write down one thing you learn from each passage:

    - Zechariah 3:1-5

    - Revelation 12:9-11

    - John 8:44

    - 2 Corinthians 11:13-15

3. The better we know God's Word, the better able we are to be sober, vigilant, and resist the enemy. Read each Scripture reference below and write out practical ways you can continue to stand and resist:

    - 1 John 2:18-27

    - 1 John 4:1-6

    - Ephesians 6:10-13

    - James 4:7

4. Peter ends his letter on a positive note and reminds us all that God is in complete control and knows it all. What a joy! What a grace! Write down the specifics of the hope that is yours in 1 Peter 5:10-11 and turn it into a prayer of gratitude.

Your Daily Gratitude List:

Week Five: DAY FIVE

We have spent five weeks journeying through Peter's letter to the church that outlines our living hope through our inheritance of Jesus Christ.

You will note that you did not do a SOAP devotional study method this week. Instead, you are asked to end your study by doing two specific things:

1. Memorize 1 Peter 5:10:

    "But may the God of all grace, who called us to His eternal glory by Christ Jesus, after you have suffered a while, perfect, establish, strengthen and settle you."

2. Go back through all of 1 Peter and with a different color highlighter or colored pencil, underline the following:

    - Red-what God, Jesus, and the Spirit have done/will do
    - Green-your identity in Jesus Christ
    - Blue-Imperatives for living

You have spent time in each chapter and this exercise will serve as a great review for you and solidify the lessons you have gleaned from your time in this book.

YOUR DAILY GRATITUDE LIST:

May God add His blessing to your time in His Word!

Works Cited

Aging with Grace; Flourishing in an anti-aging culture. Sharon W Betters and Susan Hunt. Crossway books, 2021.

Heaven Opened; the correspondence of Mary Winslow. Mary Winslow. Reformation Heritage books, 2001.

Prayers that avail much; Scriptural prayers for your daily breakthrough. Germaine Copeland. Harrison House books, 2019.

The New Spirit Filled Life Bible. New King James Version. Thomas Nelson Bibles, 2002.

The Wiersbe Bible Commentary New Testament. Colorado Springs, CO. David C. Cook Publishing, 2007. Print.

Flourish Through the Word is a community of women of all ages who gather weekly to worship, pray, study the Bible together, and build relationships. From these weekly gatherings, women are then equipped to move out into their arenas of influence and be a light for Jesus.

Flourish is a **501C3** ministry that is supported by the material fees charged for the studies and private donations. If you'd like to find out more about the ministry or make a tax-deductible donation, please visit **flourishthroughtheword.com**. Donations can be made online or by mailing a check to:

Flourish Through the Word
2020 Maltby Road, PMB 240
Bothell, WA 98021

On our website are various Bible study teaching sessions based on the studies our community has done together. These are easily viewed for use in home, church, or small group. Please contact our ministry for more details.

Flourish is delighted to provide a podcast that features Marjie and her sister, Leigh, plus guests. Each short podcast highlights topics that pertain to the daily lives of women as they seek to honor Jesus with every aspect of their lives. Find us at **flourishthroughtheword.com** and stay tuned for new epidsodes regularly.

ABOUT THE AUTHOR

Marjie Schaefer believes the Word of God is relevant, powerful, transformational, and life-giving to every single human being on the planet. She has spent her adult life investing in others and inviting them to join her in this pursuit of deeper truth. Marjie has published several studies available on Amazon: ***Life Upon Life, Come to the Table, Dare to Believe, Your Story Matters, Choose Joy, I Believe in the Name of Jesus,*** and several others.

Marjie and her husband Steve, live in the Seattle area and have four grown children, a daughter-in-law and grandson, Jack.

www.ingramcontent.com/pod-product-compliance
Lightning Source LLC
Chambersburg PA
CBHW081406070526
44583CB00020B/2701